for

thank you Jesus

for transforming my life

written and illustrated by Darcy Jackson

Published by Fictitious Ink Publishing,
Tumbler Ridge, BC, Canada, V0C 2W0

This booklet is
devoted to Lord Jesus
and dedicated to
my sister Debra.
I hope the messages
bring you strength and peace.
I love you,
Darcy

1 Peter 1:8, 9

Though you have not seen Him,
you love Him; and even though you
do not see Him now, you believe in
Him and are filled with an
inexpressible and glorious joy, for
you are receiving the goal of
your faith, the salvation of your
souls!

Thankyou Jesus for saving my soul

Lamentations 3: 22, 23
Because of the Lord's great love,
we are not consumed; for His
compassions never fail. They are
new every morning; great is
Your faithfulness!

Thankyou Jesus for each new morning.

1 John 4: 9, 10
God is love. This is how God showed His love among us: He sent His One and Only Son into the world that we might live through Him. This is love: not that we loved God, but that He loved us and sent His Son as an atoning sacrifice for our sins.

Thankyou Jesus for Your sacrifice for me.

7

John 14: 27
"Peace I leave with you; My peace I give you. I do not give to you as the world gives. Do not let your hearts be troubled and do not be afraid!"

John 16: 33
"I have told you these things, so that in Me you may have peace. In this world you will have trouble. But take heart! I have overcome the world!"

Thankyou Jesus for Your
Peace that You give to my soul.

John 8: 12
"I AM the Light of the world.
Whoever follows Me will never
walk in darkness, but will have
the Light of Life!

Thank you Jesus,
You are the Light in my
world!

John 1: 4, 5
In Him was Life, and that Life was
the Light of men. The Light shines in
the darkness, but the darkness has not
overcome it!

Psalm 112: 4
Even in darkness Light dawns for the
upright. For the Lord is gracious and
compassionate and righteous.

Thank you Jesus
Your Light overcomes
darkness

2 Corinthians 5: 17

Therefore, if anyone is in Christ, he is a new creation; the old has gone, the new has come! All this is from God, who reconciled us to Himself through Christ and gave us the ministry of reconciliation: that God was reconciling the world to Himself in Christ, not counting our sins against us.

Thankyou Jesus
I am a new creation in You

My old life is passed away

15

Psalm 46: 10
"Be still, and know that I AM
God."

Philippians 4: 4
Rejoice in the Lord always. Again
I say: Rejoice! Let your gentleness
be evident to all. The Lord is near!

James 4:8
Come near to God and He will
come near to you.

Thankyou Jesus for Your
Presence in my quiet moments.

Proverbs 18: 24
There is a Friend who sticks closer
than a brother.

John 15: 14 & 17
"You are My friends if you do
what I command… This is my
command: Love each other."

*Thankyou Jesus for being
my friend when I feel lonely*

Hebrews 7 : 24, 25
Because Jesus lives forever, He has
a permanent priesthood. Therefore
He is able to save completely and
forever, those who come to God
through Him, because He always
lives to intercede for them.

Thankyou Jesus for being my Savior

21

Acts 3: 19
Repent then, and turn to God, so
that your sins may be wiped out;
that times of refreshing may come
from the Lord.

Thankyou Jesus for the refreshing!

Psalm 93: 1
The Lords reigns, He is robed in
Majesty; the Lord is robed in
Majesty and is armed with
strength.

Hebrews 1: 3
The Son is the radiance of God's
glory and the exact representation
of His being, sustaining all things
by His powerful Word.

Thankyou Jesus for the beauty in Your Majesty!

Jeremiah 29: 11
"For I know the plans I have for you," declares the Lord, "plans to prosper you and not to harm you, plans to give you hope and a future."

Thankyou Jesus that You have plans for my life: to give me Hope and a Future

Romans 8: 28
And we know that in all things,
God works for the good of those who
love Him; who have been called
according to His purpose.

Thankyou Jesus that You cause all things to work together for my good!

Revelation 21: 1,....4

Then I saw a new heaven and a new
earth, for the first heaven and the first
earth had passed away,... And I heard a
loud voice from the throne saying, "Now
the dwelling of God is with men, and He
will live with them. They will be His
people, and God Himself will be with
them and be their God. He will wipe every
tear from their eyes. There will be no
more death or mourning or crying or
pain, for the old order of things has
passed away."

Thankyou Jesus for a place called Home.

Mathew 6: 12

Forgive us our debts, as we also
have forgiven our debtors.

Thankyou Jesus for paying my debt in full

33

Colossians 2: 13 - 15
When you were dead in your sins,
God made you alive with Christ. He
forgave us all our sins, having
cancelled the written code, with its
regulations, that was against us and
that stood opposed to us. He took it
away, nailing it to the cross. And
having disarmed the powers and
authorities, He made a public
spectacle of them, triumphing over
them by the cross!

Thankyou Jesus for forgiving me. Amen

35

Luke 2: 14
Glory to God in the highest, and
on earth peace to men on whom
His favour rests.

Thankyou Jesus: heaven is where You are.

Philippians 4: 6, 7
Do not be anxious about any-
thing, but in everything, by
prayer and petition, with thanks-
giving, present your requests to
God. And the peace of God, which
transcends all understanding, will
guard your hearts and your
minds in Christ Jesus.

Thankyou Jesus for Your Peace beyond my understanding

John 7: 37, 38
"If a man is thirsty, let him come to Me and drink. Whoever believes in Me, as Scripture has said, streams of living water will flow from within him".

Thankyou Jesus for your streams of Living Water: Your Holy Spirit in me!

The Lord is my shepherd,
I lack nothing.
He makes me lie down in
green pastures,
He leads me beside quiet waters,
He refreshes my soul.
He guides me along the right paths
for His name's sake.
Even though I walk
through the darkest valley,
I will fear no evil,
for You are with me;
Your rod and Your staff,
they comfort me.
You prepare a table before me
in the presence of my enemies.
You anoint my head with oil;
my cup overflows.
Surely your goodness and love will follow me
all the days of my life,
and I will dwell in the house of the Lord
forever.
Psalm 23
NIV

More in the series!

We hope you found this inspirational pocketbook uplifting. The simple affirmative statements, illustrations, and scriptures were prayerfully compiled by the author to bring you strength and peace.

Plus, there are more books in the series! They'd make a beautiful gift for someone you love. Available at select bookstores and online. God bless!

If you enjoyed this book, please consider leaving a positive rating or review.

www.ingramcontent.com/pod-product-compliance
Lightning Source LLC
Chambersburg PA
CBHW040905120626
46551CB00006B/654